Dessert

Coloring Book

By Mona Scot

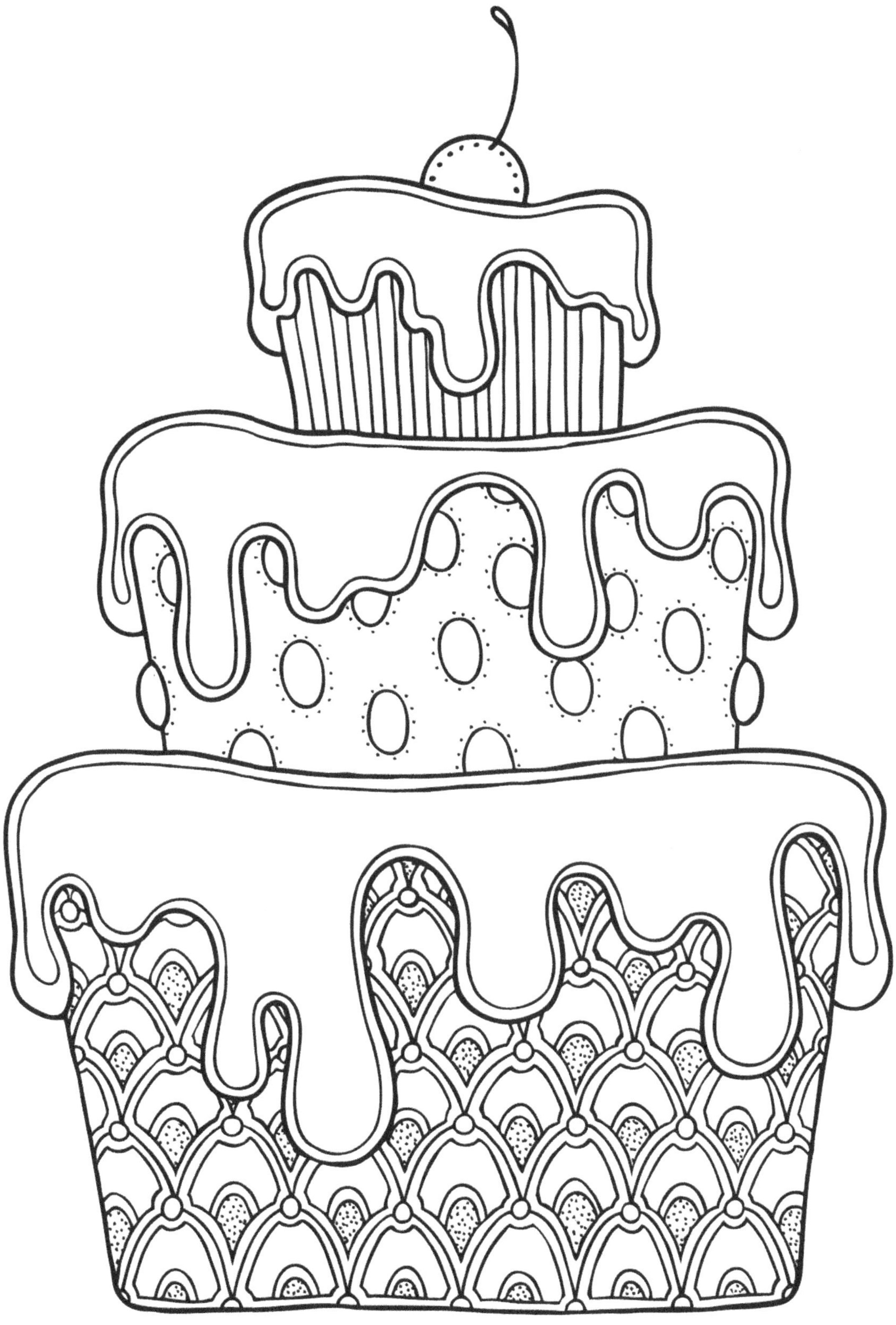

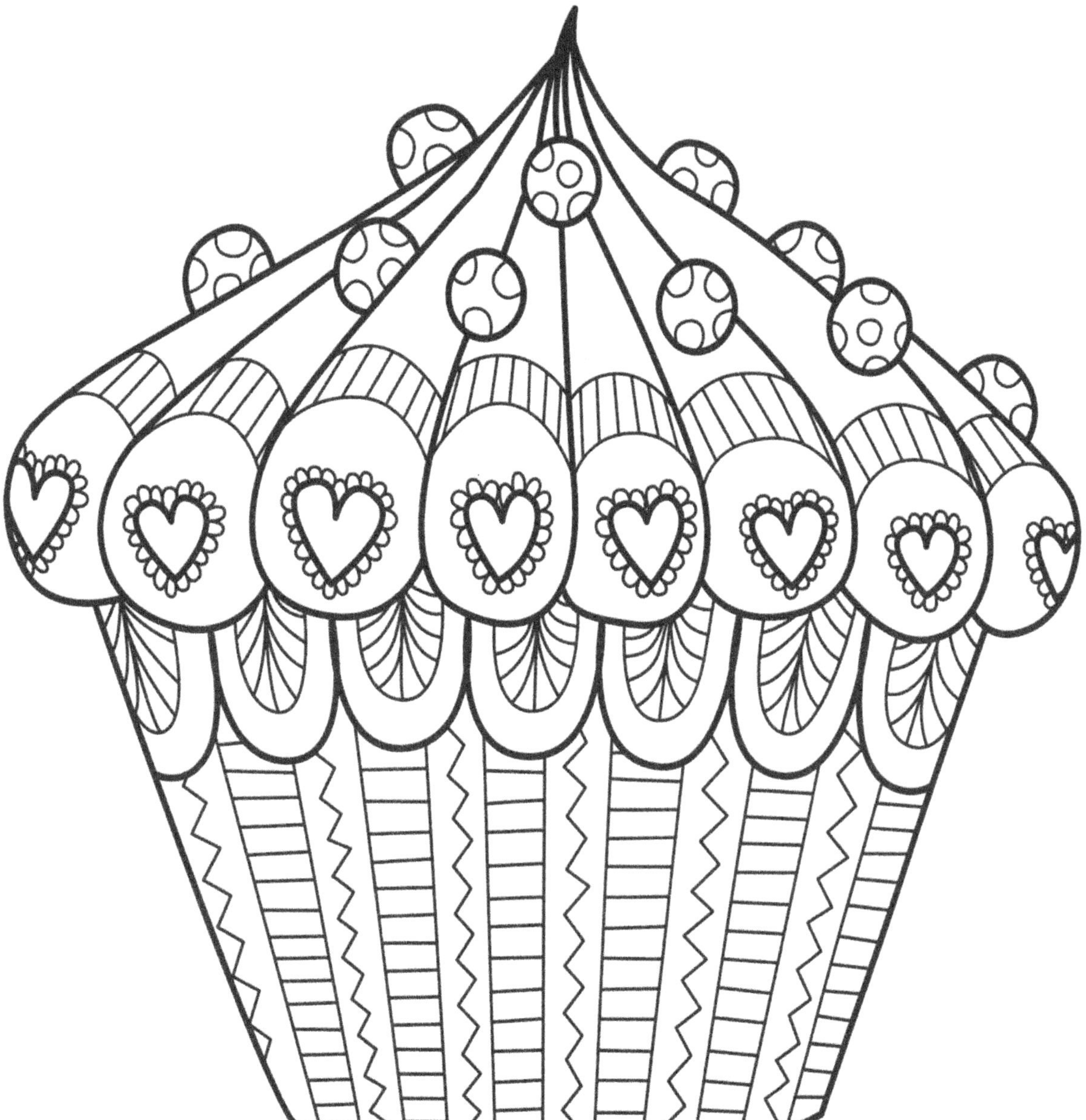

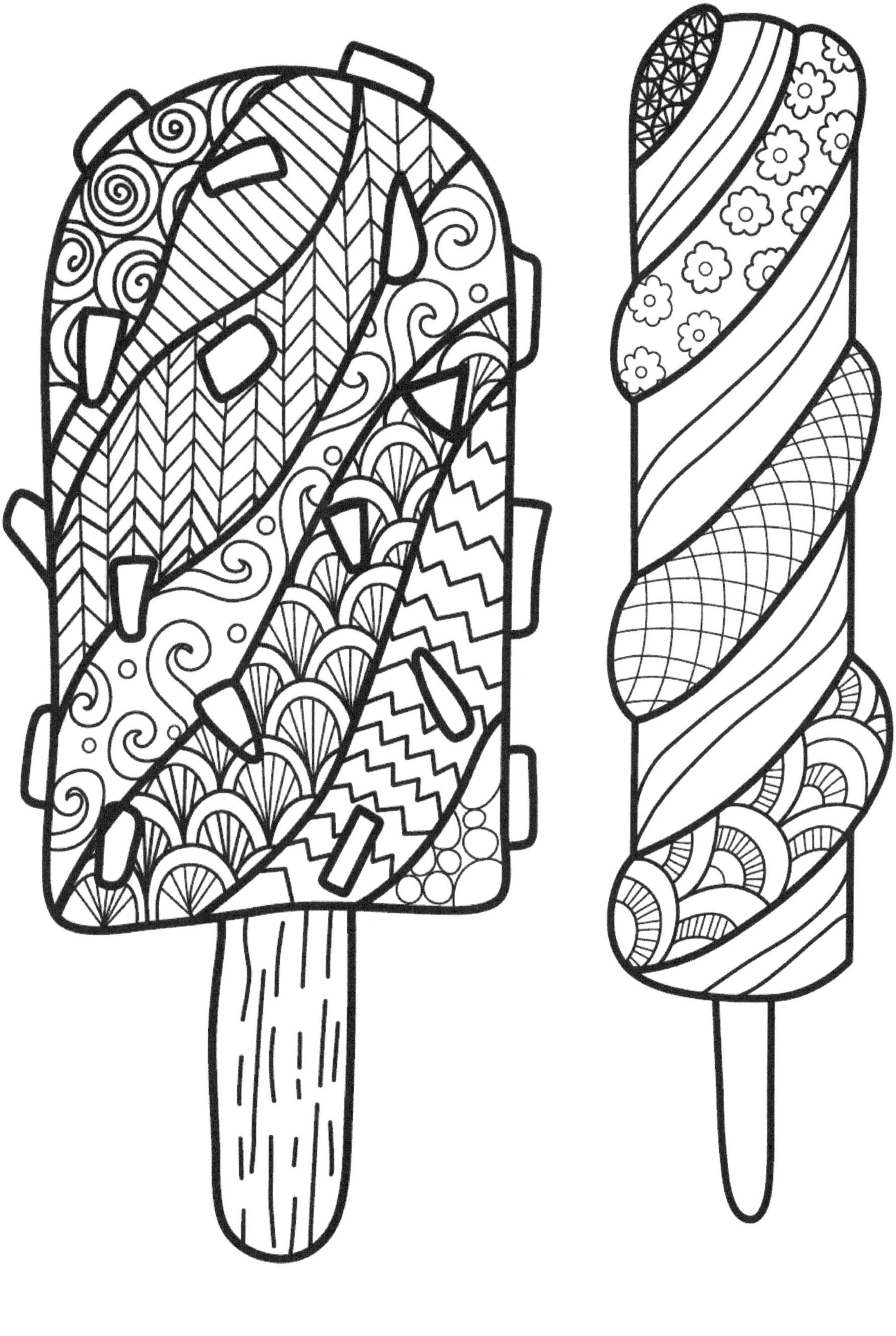

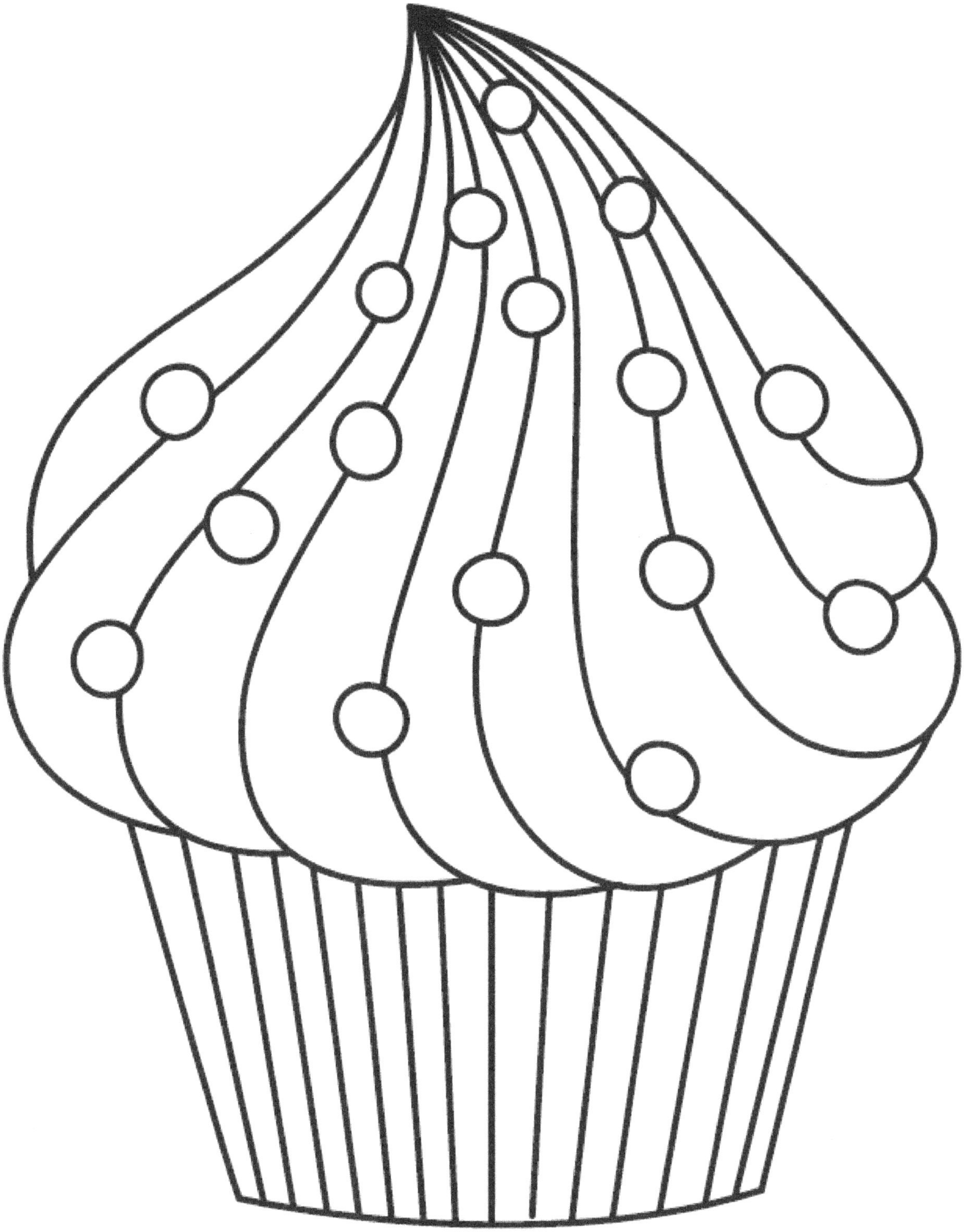

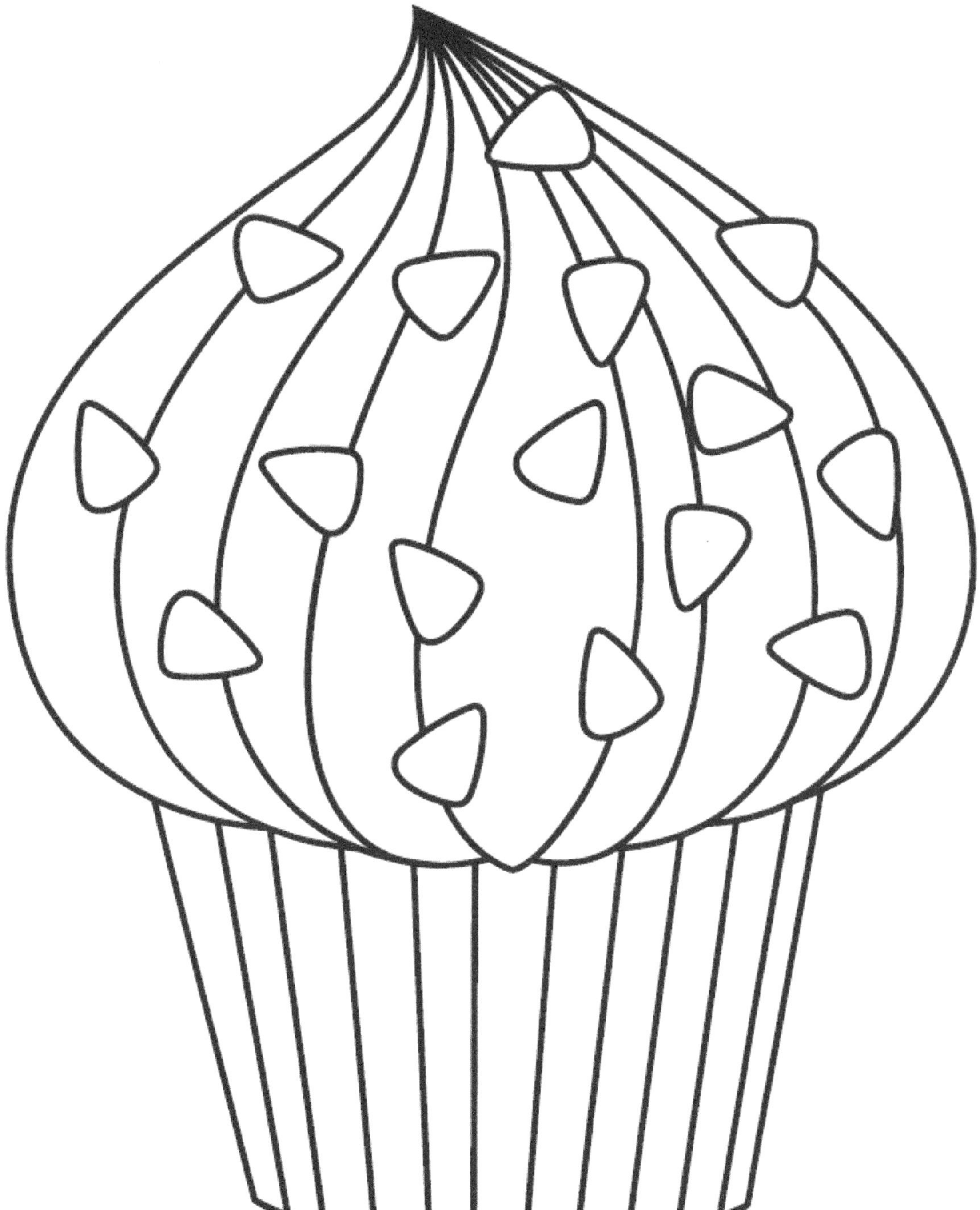

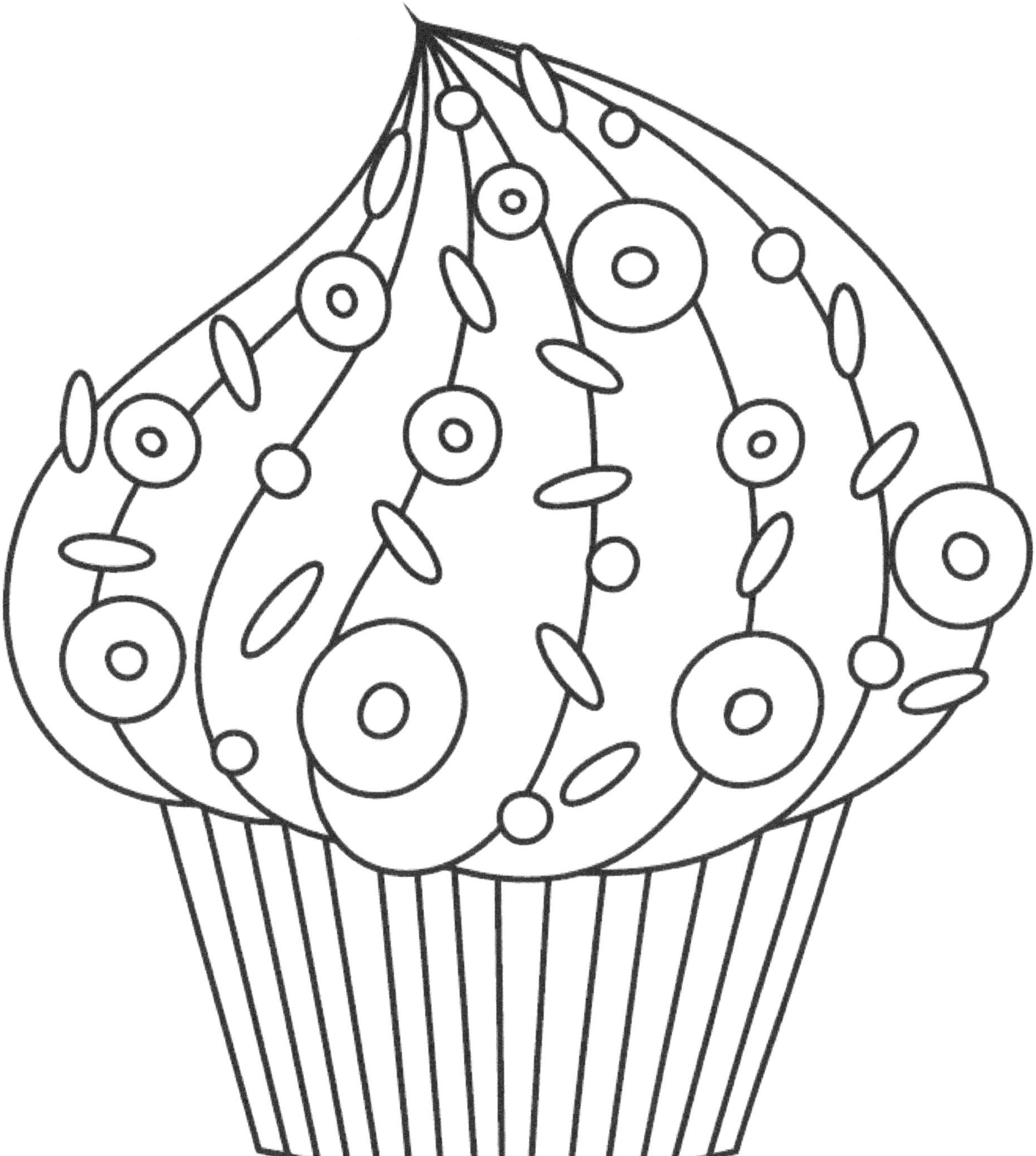

Made in the USA
Coppell, TX
14 March 2022

74958639R00057